pond plants
& cultivation

pond plants
& cultivation

Philip Swindells

Interpet Publishing

Published by Interpet Publishing,
Vincent Lane, Dorking,
Surrey RH4 3YX, England

ISBN 1-903098-33-5

Editor: Philip de Ste. Croix
Designer: Philip Clucas MSIAD
Studio photography: Neil Sutherland
Production management: Consortium,
    Poslingford, Suffolk
Print production: Leefung-Asco Printers
    Trading Ltd, China
Printed and bound in China

THE AUTHOR

Philip Swindells is a water gardening specialist with a
long experience of growing aquatic plants in many
parts of the world. He trained at the University of
Cambridge Botanic Garden and the famous aquatic
nursery of Perrys of Enfield, and ultimately became
Curator of Harlow Carr Botanical Gardens, Harrogate.
The author of many publications on water gardening,
Philip was also formerly the editor of the *Water Garden
Journal* of the International Waterlily Society who in
1994 inducted him into their Hall of Fame. He was
awarded a Mary Hellier Scholarship in 1990 by the
International Plant Propagator's Society for pioneering
work on the propagation of waterlilies.

Acknowledgements
The publishers would like to thank the
following people for their much appreciated
help and advice during the preparation of this
book: Anthony Archer-Wills, Gail Paterson and
Emma Spicer at New Barn Aquatic Nurseries,
West Chiltington, and Gill Page at Murrells
Nursery, Pulborough, West Sussex.

contents

introduction

Pond plants are amongst the most interesting that the gardener can grow, not only for their diversity, but for the effect which they can have upon the aquatic environment. The floating foliage of waterlilies and other deep-water aquatics along with that of the various free-floating aquatics provides continuing interest in the pool, but perhaps more importantly also shade beneath the water. This helps to reduce the impact of algal growth and at the same time provides a restful haven for fish. A pond should never be shaded from above, for all pond plants benefit from full uninterrupted sunlight, but this stipulation does not need to extend beneath the water.

Indeed beneath the water all manner of activity is going on. The shade produced by floating foliage, provided that it does not cover more than half the surface, permits the submerged plants to continue growing, but reduces the activity of algae, especially the single-celled green algae which sometimes produce a green pea-soup effect in the pond. It is the submerged plants which are the workhorses though, for by competing with algae for the mineral salts in the water, they effectively starve out suspended algae. This is a crucial factor in creating and maintaining a natural balance.

The submerged plants are the unsung heroes of the water garden, but they look anything but heroic. Most are fairly modest, weedy, foliage plants with poor or insignificant flowers. The only exceptions are the water violet, *Hottonia palustris* and the water crowfoot, *Ranunculus aquatilis*. Both produce lovely blossoms above the water and are a joy to behold.

It is the marginal aquatics and bog garden plants which make the major floral contribution to the water garden, although few would deny the exceptional beauty of the floating blossoms of the waterlilies, even though they are only present for the summer months. Both marginal and bog garden plants have little impact upon the well-being and natural behaviour of the garden pool. They are the plants which provide both decoration and occasionally spectacle. They provide a long season of colour from the tiny pink-flowered *Primula rosea* of early spring and the contrasting golden hummocks of marsh marigolds to the coppery-bronze hues of the royal fern, *Osmunda regalis*, as it wears its autumnal tints.

Irrespective of your water garden, there are plants to fulfil your needs. For a tub on a terrace there are the pygmy waterlilies and the dwarf Japanese reedmace, while the large pond can be served by the gigantic waterlily *Nymphaea* 'Gladstoneana' and dressed with reedmace and yellow flag. There is truly something for everyone.

Above: Nymphaea 'Firecrest', a popular waterlily for the medium-sized pond.
Right: Planted perfection. The verdant pads and colourful blossoms of
waterlilies surrounded by open water. The poolside is thronged and framed
with plants which tie it to its surroundings..

pygmy and small waterlilies

While most gardeners are familiar with traditional waterlilies that grow in garden pools, there is also a range of pygmy and small-growing varieties that can be grown in tubs, containers and sinks. These can all be cultivated in the larger pond as well, providing the depth is suitable, true pygmy kinds often occupying positions on the marginal shelves.

The small-growing varieties of our familiar waterlilies have the same life-style as the larger kinds. However, the pygmy varieties can be treated differently. While most waterlilies require constant emersion in water in order to grow and prosper, the pygmy kinds can be removed and stored in damp conditions for the winter. This means that a tub which accommodates a pygmy waterlily all summer need not remain as a container full of water for the inactive six months of each year. Water can be drained from the tub and the waterlily kept damp in its compost until the spring when water is added and once again it grows away strongly.

Pygmy waterlilies can also be grown very successfully in rock pools providing that there is no water flowing through them. As winter approaches, drain off the pool, fill it with straw and cover tightly with perspex or polythene. The waterlilies will overwinter well and the risk of damage to the rock pool from the small body of water freezing solid and expanding will be eliminated. If this is considered unsightly, a pool heater will prevent severe freezing.

Above: *Pygmy waterlilies are complete miniature replicas of standard varieties. They have the same flowering season, which extends from early summer until autumn.*

CULTIVATION TIPS

Pygmy and small-growing varieties of waterlilies are grown in containers or baskets, although sometimes the pygmy kinds are planted directly into suitable soil or an aquatic planting compost on the bottom of small tub or planter where space is restricted.

They are all easy going, requiring repotting and replanting every three years and fertilizing regularly during the seasons between. Propagation is by division or eyes, and in the case of *N.* 'Pygmaea Alba', seed as well.

Below: Nymphaea *'Pygmaea Helvola' is very prolific.*

Above: All waterlilies must have full uninterrupted sunlight if they are to prosper. With pygmy and small-growing varieties, it is important to top up the pool or container regularly with water to replace that lost to evaporation. Neglecting to do this will result in a rapid deterioration of the plants.

RECOMMENDED VARIETIES

Nymphaea 'Graziella'
Orange-red flowers up to 5cm (2in) across with deep orange stamens are produced in abundance throughout the summer. The olive-green leaves are blotched with brown and purple. Spread: 30-60cm (1-2ft). Depth: 30-60cm (1-2ft). Flowering period: summer. Propagation: eyes.

N. 'Hermine'
Tulip-shaped blossoms of the purest white are held above the dark green oval foliage. Spread: 30-60cm (1-2ft). Depth 30-60cm (1-2ft). Flowering period: summer. Propagation: eyes.

N. 'Pygmaea Alba'
The tiniest of waterlilies with blossoms no more than 2.5cm (1in) across. These are pure white, star-shaped and of a delicate papery texture. Small dark green 'lily pads with purple

reverses. Spread: 20cm (8in). Depth: up to 20cm (8in). Flowering period: summer. Propagation: eyes.

N. 'Pygmaea Helvola'
Beautiful star-like canary-yellow flowers are produced throughout the summer amongst olive green foliage which is heavily mottled with purple and brown. Spread: 30cm (1ft). Depth up to 30cm (1ft). Flowering period: summer. Propagation: eyes.

N. 'William Falconer'
Blood red flowers with bright yellow stamens are produced amongst deep olive green 'lily pads which in their early stages of growth are a distinctive purplish hue. Spread: 45-60cm (1½-2ft). Depth 45-60cm (1½-2ft). Flowering period: summer. Propagation: eyes.

'PROBLEM' VARIETIES

While white and yellow pygmy waterlilies are free-flowering and well worth growing, the red ones are a big disappointment. *Nymphaea* 'Pygmaea Rubra' and *N.* 'Pygmaea Rubis' produce small numbers of flowers and very few manage to come out at the same time. Both varieties are difficult to propagate as they produce eyes sparingly and unlike *N.* 'Pygmaea Alba' which can be readily increased from seed, the few flowers that these varieties produce are sterile and so seed is not an option.

medium-sized waterlilies

There is a wonderful array of waterlilies available for the gardener with the average-sized garden pond. Most of these are much-loved older varieties produced in France during the latter part of the 19th century and the early part of the 20th century. All have a long history of cultivation and are reliable in most climates, unlike some of the modern untested kinds which originate in the United States and find life difficult in the cooler and wetter areas of northern Europe.

Waterlilies are available in a wide range of colours, only blue and smoky green being found in tropical varieties but not amongst the hardies. Flower shapes vary from star-like in 'Rose Arey' to peony-shaped with 'James Brydon' and cup-shaped with 'Marliacea Albida'. Unlike the tropical varieties which raise their flowers above the water, most of those of the hardy kinds float on the surface of the water amongst the waterlily pads.

All the medium-sized waterlilies popularly offered for sale are completely winter hardy. Their size varies according to the depth at which they are growing, the shallower the water the smaller the surface spread of foliage.

The greatest diversity of flower shapes, colour, fragrance and leaf patterns are to be found among the older, more traditional medium-sized varieties of waterlily.

Above: Nymphaea *'James Brydon' is the best peony-shaped flowered waterlily available, although it does take a season to settle down into a regular flowering pattern.*

RECOMMENDED VARIETIES

Nymphaea 'Arc-en-ciel'
The only truly variegated foliage variety of waterlily. The leaves are deep olive green boldly splashed with purple, rose, white and bonze. The flowers have narrow petals and are pink and papery. Spread: 45-90cm (1½-3ft). Depth: 45-90cm (1½-3ft). Flowering period: summer. Propagation: eyes.

N. 'Gloire de Temple-sur-Lot'
A fully double, fragrant, rose-pink flowered waterlily which has the appearance of a chrysanthemum rather than a waterlily. Large plain green leaves.
Spread: 45-90cm (1½-3ft). Depth: 45-90cm (1½-3ft). Flowering period: summer. Propagation: eyes.

N. 'James Brydon'
A wonderful crimson-flowered waterlily with rounded blossoms rather like those of a peony. Dark purplish-green leaves which are often flecked with maroon.
Spread: 45-90cm (1½-3ft). Depth: 45-90cm (1½-3ft). Flowering period: summer. Propagation: eyes.

N. 'Marliacea Albida'
Fragrant pure white cup-shaped blossoms up to 15cm (6in) across. The sepals and reverse of the petals are often flushed with pink. The leaves are dark green with purplish undersides. Spread: 45-90cm (1½-3ft). Depth: 45-90cm (1½-3ft). Flowering period: summer. Propagation: eyes.

N. 'Marliacea Chromatella'
Large canary yellow blossoms with broad petals. The sepals are pale yellow and flushed with pink. The olive green foliage is distinctively splashed and stained with maroon and bronze. Spread: 45-75cm (1½-2½ft). Depth: 45-75cm (1½-2½ft). Flowering period: summer. Propagation: eyes.

N. 'Rose Arey'
Large star-like rose-pink blossoms with a wonderful aniseed fragrance. The juvenile leaves are red and the adult green leaves often have a distinctive reddish flush. Spread: 45-75cm (1½-2½ft). Depth: 45-75cm (1½-2½ft). Flowering period: summer. Propagation: eyes.

Above: Nymphaea odorata *'Alba' is a very hardy and free-flowering fragrant waterlily variety with attractive apple-green foliage.*

'PROBLEM' VARIETIES

There is only one medium-sized waterlily to avoid and that is *N.* 'Col. A.J. Welch'. This is a sparsely flowered yellow variety which reproduces viviparously. Often what appears to be a promising bud turns out to be a plantlet. As it reproduces so freely, it is often offered cheaply in garden centres. It is in any event a rather vigorous and coarse-growing variety with an excess of foliage.

Left: Nymphaea *'Marliacea Chromatella' is a most reliable and free-flowering waterlily for the medium-sized pool. It is very versatile and will continue to prosper in as little as 30cm (12in) of water or as much as 1 metre (40in), which is why it is so widely available from garden centres.*

large waterlilies

There are a number of magnificent large waterlilies which are only well suited to the farm pond or lake. For most gardeners the cultivation of these beautiful aquatics is out of the question, but it is important to know which varieties are suited to large expanses of water as they are often offered for sale to home gardeners for average-sized garden pools. They will grow in shallower water of course, but the flowers and foliage will not develop to the full.

Large-growing waterlilies are not very suitable for cultivating in baskets. They are much too vigorous. They grow much more freely when allowed to roam around the pool floor. When growing happily, varieties like *N.* 'Gladstoneana' and *N.* 'Escarboucle' can produce spectacular blossoms up to 25cm (10in) across and individual 'lily pads' as much as 30cm (1ft) in diameter. When growing these giants allow between 2m (6½ft) and 3m (10ft) of surface area to be covered by the foliage of each plant. None will grow freely in less than 1.2m (4ft) of water.

Below: Of the various strong-growing purple and plum-coloured varieties with white streaking, it is Nymphaea *'Charles de Meurville' which has the longest flowering season.*

···· RECOMMENDED VARIETIES ····

Nymphaea 'Charles de Meurville'

A vigorous grower with large plum-coloured blossoms, the petals of which are tipped and streaked with white. The flowers darken to deep wine with age. The foliage is deep olive green. Spread: 1.2-1.8m (4-6ft). Depth: 1.2-1.8m (4-6ft). Flowering period: summer. Propagation: eyes.

N. 'Escarboucle'

A very large-flowered, richly fragrant crimson variety with a centre of bright yellow stamens. Immense bright green 'lily pads. Spread: 1.2-1.8m (4-6ft). Depth: 1.2-1.8m (4-6ft). Flowering period: summer. Propagation: eyes.

N. 'Gladstoneana'

Enormous pure white waxy blossoms with centres of bold yellow stamens. Dark green leaves with leaf stalks speckled brown. Spread: 1.2-2.4m (4-8ft). Depth: 1.2-2.4m (4-8ft). Flowering period: summer. Propagation: eyes.

N. 'Marliacea Carnea'

Flesh-pink vanilla-scented blossoms with bright yellow stamens are produced in abundance amongst plain green foliage which is often purplish when it first emerges. Newly planted specimens sometimes produce white flowers during the first season. Spread: 1.2-1.8m (4-6ft). Depth: 1.2-1.8m (4-6ft). Flowering period: summer. Propagation: eyes.

N. tuberosa 'Richardsonii'

Startling white waxy, globular blossoms are produced amongst the brightest green rounded foliage. Each blossom has distinctive bright pea-green sepals. Spread: 1.2-1.5m (4-5ft). Depth: 1.2-1.5m (4-5ft). Flowering period: summer. Propagation: eyes.

Above: Nymphaea *'Escarboucle'* is one of the most versatile large-growing waterlilies. When given an unrestricted root run and a generous depth of water, it proves itself to be truly the queen of aquatics with individual blossoms the size of soup dishes.

Left: Nymphaea *'Marliacea Carnea'* is probably the most widely cultivated pink flowered waterlily. Raised by the famous French hybridizer Joseph Bory Latour Marliac, it is also erroneously sold under the name of 'Morning Glory'.

other deep-water aquatics

While the deeper area of the pool unquestionably belongs to the waterlilies, there are occasions when the introduction of other deep-water aquatics can be of great benefit. The two most valuable attributes of those plants referred to by the nurseryman as deep-water aquatics are their tolerance of moving water and seasonality of display.

Unless the pool is very large it is impossible to grow a waterlily successfully when either a fountain or waterfall are introduced. Waterlilies are natural inhabitants of quiet backwaters and go into a rapid decline when subjected to water flow or constant splashing on the foliage. The nuphars

Above: *The water hawthorn,* Aponogeton distachyos, *is not only a floral delight, but a culinary delicacy. The crispy white flowers are an excellent addition to salads.*

or pond lilies can take their place, being tolerant of both moving water and a little shade. They produce floating foliage that is very similar to a waterlily, but one has to concede that the flowers are not as spectacular.

With the water hawthorn, *Aponogeton distachyos*, the foliage is smaller and not as effective, but the blossoms are superb, being vanilla-scented and produced from late spring until the approach of winter. This is a much longer flowering season than any waterlily.

Aponogeton distachyos (Water hawthorn)

A wonderful plant with a flowering season which extends from late spring until the approach of winter. The blossoms are forked white with black stamens, and have a delicious vanilla fragrance. The more or less oblong green leaves are often splashed with maroon. Spread: 30-90cm (1-3ft). Depth: 30-90cm (1-3ft). Flowering period: late spring to winter. Propagation: division/seed.

Nuphar advena (American spatterdock)

A strong-growing pond lily with globular yellow blossoms 8cm (3in) across. These are often tinged with purple and have bright coppery-red stamens. The large fresh green 'lily pads are thick and leathery. Spread: 45cm-1.5m (1½-5ft). Depth: 45cm-1.5m (1½-5ft). Flowering period: summer. Propagation: division.

N. lutea (Yellow pond lily)

Small bottle-shaped yellow flowers with a distinctive alcoholic aroma are produced amongst leathery fresh green oval leaves. A vigorous plant which is best suited to the larger pool. Spread: 30cm-2.4m (1-8ft). Depth: 30cm-2.4m (1-8ft). Flowering period: summer. Propagation: division.

Nymphoides peltata (Water fringe)

This vigorous-growing plant at first glance looks like a pygmy waterlily. It has bright yellow fringed blossoms which are produced freely from midsummer until early autumn amongst small rounded, bright green miniature 'lily pads which are often liberally splashed with brown. Spread: 30-75cm (1-2½ft). Depth: 30-75cm (1-2½ft). Flowering period: midsummer to autumn. Propagation: division.

Orontium aquaticum (Golden club)

A curious relative of the arum lily which produces masses of upright pencil-like blossoms in bright gold and white. The blue-green foliage is lance-shaped and floats on the surface of the water. Spread: 45cm (1½ft). Depth: up to 45cm (1½ft). Flowering period: summer. Propagation: division.

Opposite page: Nymphoides peltata *is a very adaptable plant tolerating moving water and partial shade.*

Above: Orontium aquaticum *is amongst the hardiest and finest free-flowering deep-water aquatics.*

reeds and rushes

Apart from waterlilies most people would regard reeds and rushes as the next most typical plants of a pond. Especially the typhas or reedmaces with their thick chocolate-coloured fruiting spikes which are popularly referred to as bulrushes.

Reeds and rushes are amongst the most difficult plants to grow successfully in a garden pool. Most are not too fond of cultivation in a basket unless kept well fertilized.

If let loose in the soil on the margins of a pool they spread rapidly and grow into one another. Providing that their behaviour is well understood, however, they can be satisfactorily cultivated and make a major contribution to the visual aspect of a pool.

All have architectural qualities, which in the case of the *Juncus* or true rushes, persist all year long. The scirpus or *Schoenoplectus* are almost evergreen too and add much with their often startlingly bold foliage. Flowers are the least important characteristic of most reeds and rushes, except for the flowering rush, *Butomus umbellatus*, a magnificent plant, which in late summer produces the loveliest pink blossoms.

Below: *The poker-like heads of the lesser reedmace,* Typha angustifolia, *are much admired. However, the plant is very invasive and must be contained within a planting basket or restricted by water depth when planted directly into the margins.*

Right: *Sweet galingale,* Cyperus longus, *is happiest when established on a bank and allowed to colonize mud at the water's edge.*

RECOMMENDED VARIETIES

Butomus umbellatus (Flowering rush)
Not a true rush, but the foliage is bright green
and rush-like. Showy pink blossoms are produced
on spreading umbels during late summer.
Height: 60-90cm (2-3ft). Spread: 30-45cm
(1-1½ft). Depth: up to 15cm (6in). Flowering
period: late summer. Propagation: division.

Carex pendula (Pendulous sedge)
One of the few sedges which are worth
growing in the pool. A tall handsome plant
with broad green strap-like leaves and long
drooping brownish-green catkin-like flowers
during summer. Height: 90cm-1.2m (3-4ft).
Spread: 45-60cm (1½-2ft). Depth up to
10cm (4in). Flowering period: summer.
Propagation: division/seed.

**Juncus effusus 'Spiralis' (Corkscrew
rush)** A bizarre version of the common soft
rush but with dark green needle-like leaves
which are twisted and contorted like a
corkscrew. A great novelty which produces
small brown tassels of flowers. Height: 30-
45cm (1-1½ft). Spread 15-25cm (6-10in).
Depth: up to 15cm (6in). Flowering period:
summer. Propagation: division.

**Schoenoplectus tabernaemontani
'Zebrinus' (Zebra rush)** A startling mutant
plant with thick long needle-like stems which
are alternately banded horizontally with white
and green. Occasional small tassels of brown
flowers are produced. Height: 90cm-1.2m
(3-4ft). Spread: 45-60cm (1½-2ft). Depth: up
to 15cm (6in). Flowering period: summer.
Propagation: division.

Typha minima (Dwarf Japanese bulrush)
This wonderful dwarf rush produces masses
of dark green needle-like foliage amongst
which chunky rounded brown fruiting heads
are produced. Height: 45cm (18in). Spread:
15-20cm (6-8in). Depth: up to 10cm (4in).
Flowering period: summer.
Propagation: division.

*Below: Reeds and rushes make an important visual and functional
contribution to the pool and provide a wonderful habitat for wildlife.*

'PROBLEM' VARIETIES

Avoid all species of plain green **Juncus, Carex** and the smaller leaf **Schoenoplectus.**
These are weedy species which seed themselves freely and can swamp a pond.
A number, such as **Juncus effusus** and **Carex riparia**, are offered by nurserymen and
garden centres for wildlife ponds, but they should be avoided as they can become really
pernicious and create serious maintenance problems.

irises

Of all the marginal plants it is the irises that show the richest diversity. They are of varying stature and have flowers of almost every colour and combination imaginable. Outside the pond the iris family is extraordinary with tiny bulbous species for the rock garden, monster bearded kinds for the sunny herbaceous border and elegant moisture-loving varieties for the bog garden. It is the moisture-loving kind that are sometimes confused with the true water iris, for there are great similarities in appearance and not all nurserymen or garden centres know the difference.

There is a simple test which the gardener can carry out to determine whether an iris will be happy in the margins of a pond or prefer life in a bog garden. Take an iris leaf between the finger and thumb and run gently up the leaf. If the leaf is smooth, the iris will be happy standing in water. If the leaf has a strong mid-rib, then it will prefer to inhabit a bog garden.

Irises are principally grown for their beautiful blossoms which are produced freely during mid-summer, but their bold sword-like foliage can be magnificent, particularly the variegated varieties, and produce quite dramatic architectural effects, especially in the formal pool.

Left: *Yellow flag,* Iris pseudacorus, *is a marvellous plant for the larger pool or wildlife pond. It has yielded many good varieties. Apart from the creamy-yellow and green variegated 'Variegata', there is a double-flowered form 'Flore Pleno', a pale yellow variety 'Sulphur Queen', as well as the creamy-white flowered 'E. Turnipseed'.*

Right: *Irises of all kinds, irrespective of whether they are true aquatics or bog varieties, offer great opportunities for imaginative use by the water gardener.*

Iris laevigata

The parent of many of the brightly coloured aquatic iris. A handsome blue flowered plant with bold clumps of smooth green sword-like foliage. Height: 60-90cm (2-3ft). Spread: 30-45cm (1-1½ft). Depth: up to 15cm (6in). Flowering period: summer. Propagation: division/seed.

I. laevigata 'Variegata'

This plant is often sold under the name of 'Elegantissima'. It has the same beautiful blue flowers as its parent and spectacular green and white variegated sword-like foliage. Height: 60-75cm (2-2½ft). Spread: 30-40cm (1-1½ft). Depth up to 10cm (4in). Flowering period: summer. Propagation: division.

I. pseudacorus (Yellow flag)

A very well-known vigorous-growing plant for the larger water garden and wildlife pool. Tall mid-green strap-like leaves and bright yellow blossoms with conspicuous black markings. The dark green seed pods split to reveal orange-brown seeds. Height: 90cm-1.2m (3-4ft). Spread: 45-60cm (1½-2ft). Depth up to 25cm (10in). Flowering period: summer. Propagation: division/seed.

I. pseudacorus 'Variegata'

One of the most spectacular variegated foliage plants. Although producing bright yellow flowers like its parent the yellow flag, it is the handsome creamy-yellow and green striped foliage for which this plant is grown. Height: 60-75cm (2-2½ft). Spread: 30-40cm (1-1½ft). Depth: up to 15cm (6in). Flowering period: summer. Propagation: division.

I. versicolor 'Kermesina'

The most beautiful variety of the widely cultivated *Iris versicolor*. Deep plum-coloured blossoms with golden markings. Bold green sword-like leaves. Height: 60-75cm (2-2½ft). Spread: 30-40cm (1-1½ft). Depth: up to 10cm (4in). Flowering period: summer. Propagation: division.

other marginals

The poolside provides endless opportunities for growing an enormous range of interesting plants. In many cases the marginal area of the pool is devoted to plants that disguise the harsh edge and provide a seamless union to the area where garden and water meet. Plants like the scrambling brooklime, *Veronica beccabunga,* creeping jenny, *Lysimachia nummularia* or invasive water mint, *Mentha aquatica*. Such spreading characters can be punctuated with the bold foliage of the aquatic irises or dark green mounds of the marsh marigold, *Caltha palustris.*

Marginal plants can also extend the period of colour and interest in a pool. Waterlilies are really only interesting for the summer months. It is characters like the common marsh marigold, *Caltha palustris*, and its double form 'Flore Pleno' which provide spring highlights at a time when the pool is devoid of plant life and offers just a glassy stillness.

The use of selected marginal aquatics also provides an opportunity for creating a successful wildlife pool, for on the confines of a marginal shelf a surprising array of interesting plants can be accommodated adjacent to one another, each with the potential to contribute to the life cycle of a different creature.

RECOMMENDED VARIETIES

Calla palustris (Bog arum)
An excellent creeping marginal for disguising the pool edge. It has a strong creeping rootstock which is clothed in handsome glossy heart-shaped foliage. The white blossoms are like small sails and are followed during late summer by bright orange-red fruits. Height: 15-30cm (6in-1ft). Spread: 10-15cm (4-6in). Depth: up to 10cm (4in). Flowering period: summer.
Propagation: seed/division/cuttings.

Caltha palustris (Marsh marigold)
A great marginal plant for spring flowering. Dark green mounds of glossy scalloped dark green foliage are smothered in bright golden-yellow waxy saucer-shaped blossoms. Height: 30-60cm (1-2ft). Spread: 15-30cm (6in-1ft). Depth: up to 30cm (1ft), but best in 10cm (4in) of water. Flowering period: spring.
Propagation: seed/division/cuttings.

Left: Pontederia cordata *is a highlight of the late summer pool, especially when planted with the lovely pink flowering rush,* Butomus umbellatus.

RECOMMENDED VARIETIES

***Lysimachia nummularia* (Creeping jenny)** A fast-growing creeping almost evergreen plant which during summer is smothered with yellow buttercup-like flowers. Height: 2.5cm (1in). Spread: 30-45cm (1-1⅟ft). Depth: up to 10cm (4in). Will grow through water without difficulty. Flowering period: summer. Propagation: division.

***Myosotis scorpioides* (Water forget-me-not)** An aquatic and perennial version of our common bedding forget-me-not, but perennial. A hummock-forming smooth-leafed plant which for most of the summer is smothered with tiny blue starry flowers. Height: 20-25cm (8-10in). Spread: 10-15cm (4-6in). Depth: up to 10cm (4in). Flowering period: summer. Propagation: seed/division.

***Pontederia cordata* (Pickerel)** Spikes of soft blue flowers appear from amongst sheaves of glossy dark green leaves during late summer. A fine upright architectural plant. Height: 60-90cm (2-3ft). Spread: 30-45cm (1-1⅟ft). Depth: up to 15cm (6in). Flowering period: late summer. Propagation: seed/division/cuttings.

***Veronica beccabunga* (Brooklime)** Dark blue flowers with distinctive white eyes are produced in the axils of the leaves of this fast-growing evergreen scrambling aquatic. Perfect for growing to disguise the harsh edge of an artificial pond. Height: 15-20cm (6-8in). Spread: 10cm (4in). Depth: up to 10cm (4in). Flowering period: summer. Propagation: division.

Right: *Spring delights at the waterside with golden hummocks of* Caltha palustris *and the hooded spathes of* Lysichiton americanus.

floating and submerged plants

Many gardeners regard these as the least important pond plants, and from an aesthetic point of view they are the most uninteresting. However, both submerged and floating aquatics are the powerhouse of the pond's ecology. Without them the only way to maintain water clarity is with a pool filter, and for most aquatic life this is a sterile and wholly naked environment. The water may be pure, but without places for pondlife to hide, feed and reproduce, the pond becomes a furniture-less room.

The submerged plants are not very noticeable as they spend their lives rooted to the pool floor and only emerge above the surface of the water to flower. With the exception of the water violet, *Hottonia palustris,* and the water crowfoot, *Ranunculus aquatilis,* none of them produces attractive flowers and they make no visual contribution to the aquatic scene.

Floating plants are a similar proposition, although the white blossoms of both the water chestnut, *Trapa natans*, and the frogbit, *Hydrocharis morsus-ranae*, are quite pretty. It is the way in which they function together that is important – the floating plants, which reduce the light falling into the water and so lower algal activity, are complemented by the submerged plants which mop up excess nutrients that are present in the water and help to starve the algae out of existence.

FLOATING PLANTS

Hydrocharis morsus-ranae (Frogbit)
An excellent small floating plant for tub, container or small pond. Neat rosettes of mid-green kidney-shaped leaves sprinkled with three-petalled white blossoms throughout the summer.
Flowering period: summer. Propagation: division.

Stratiotes aloides (Water soldier)
This extraordinary plant looks like a narrow-leafed pineapple top floating in the water. Papery pinkish-white flowers are produced during the summer. Flowering period: summer. Propagation: division.

Trapa natans (Water chestnut)
Handsome rosettes of rhomboidal dark green floating foliage are interspersed with pretty white flowers. Towards the end of the summer spiny black nuts are produced which fall to the floor of the pool and reappear and germinate the following year.
Flowering period: summer. Propagation: division.

Utricularia vulgaris (Greater bladderwort)
Bright yellow antirrhinum-like flowers are produced on strong stems which emerge from a mass of fine green foliage which floats just beneath the surface of the water. These are interspersed with bladders which capture and digest errant aquatic insects.
Flowering period: summer. Propagation: division.

Above: *Water crowfoot,* Ranunculus aquatilis, *is one of the most attractive flowering submerged aquatics. It grows happily in both still and quickly flowing water.*

Right: *The versatile* Myriophyllum aquaticum *often takes on rich red and orange hues at the approach of autumn.*

SUBMERGED PLANTS

Hottonia palustris (Water violet)

The most beautiful of the hardy submerged aquatics. Lovely whorled bright green filigree foliage atop which during summer are produced spikes of fine whitish or lilac-flushed blossoms. Flowering period: summer. Propagation: cuttings.

Lagarosiphon major (Goldfish weed)

Almost too well-known to need description. This dark green crispy curled fish weed is widely offered by pet shops for goldfish bowls and fish tanks. The best and most efficient of all the submerged aquatics. Flowering period: summer. Propagation: cuttings.

Myriophyllum aquaticum (Parrot's feather)

A plant which can grow submerged, climb out on to the margins of the pool and even invade the bog garden. Blue-green finely-cut leaves on scrambling stems. A most versatile plant. Flowering period: summer. Propagation: cuttings.

Ranunculus aquatilis (Water crowfoot)

An excellent submerged aquatic which produces beautiful papery white and gold blossoms during summer just above the water and amongst clover-like floating leaves. The submerged foliage is deeply dissected and much loved by fish as a place to spawn. Flowering period: summer. Propagation: cuttings.

flowering bog plants

The bog garden is a wonderful adjunct to the pool for it can offer an attractive backdrop and provide interest and colour for much of the year. Even during the winter a well-placed clump of the moisture-loving, red-stemmed *Cornus alba* 'Sibirica' or a stooled specimen of the orange-stemmed willow, *Salix alba* 'Chermesina', can create height and colourful interest.

It is the flowering bog plants that produce the most lasting and startling colour, although the summer clothing of foliage on structural plants like the cornus and willow offers a wonderful backdrop and softens their harshness.

Right: Candelabra primulas and moisture-loving irises live together in tangled harmony and make a wonderful late spring and early summer display of colour in the bog garden.

Far right: Bog garden plants are also adaptable to streamside planting where they may receive periodic inundation.

Left: Candelabra primulas are easily increased from seed sown immediately it ripens. Do not allow the plants to self-seed naturally. Remove faded flower heads before seed distribution takes place.

Many bog garden plants are very brightly coloured, especially the early summer-flowering primulas like the bright crimson *Primula japonica* and vivid orange *P. aurantiaca*. Likewise the perennial lobelias such as *Lobelia cardinalis* with its scarlet blossoms and beetroot-coloured foliage and *L. vedrariensis* sporting rich violet flowers and maroon-flushed leaves.

The bog garden first comes to life in early spring with the bright pink of *Primula rosea* and the lilac and white drumsticks of *P. denticulata*. Colour and interest continues throughout the season until the last fading blossoms of the bright orange *Ligularia* 'Desdemona' fall with the arrival of autumn gales.

RECOMMENDED VARIETIES

Astilbe arendsii hybrids

These are a group of brightly coloured mid-to late summer flowering plants with dense plumes of blossoms appearing above mounds of densely cut foliage. 'Fanal' is red, 'Peach Blossom' pink and 'Irrlicht' white. Height: 45-90cm (1½-3ft). Spread: 25-45cm (10in-1½ft). Flowering period: summer. Propagation: division.

Cardamine pratensis (Cuckoo flower)

A charming spring-flowering perennial with single rosy-lilac flowers and pale green fern-like foliage. The variety 'Flore Pleno' has fully double blossoms. Height: 30-45cm (1-1½ft). Spread: 15-25cm (6-10in). Flowering period: spring. Propagation: division/seed

Filipendula ulmaria (Meadowsweet)

Frothy spires of scented creamy-white blossoms are reproduced during summer above deeply-cut foliage. There is a double flowered form called 'Flore Pleno' and a golden leafed one – 'Aurea'. Height: 60cm-1.2m (2-4ft). Spread: 30-60cm (1-2ft). Flowering period: summer. Propagation: division/seed.

Iris ensata (Clematis-flowered iris of Japan)

The finest swamp iris. The species has tufts of grassy foliage surmounted by broad-petalled deep purple blossoms during summer. There are many named varieties in a rich array of colours. Height: 60-75cm (2-2½ft). Spread: 30-40cm (1-1½ft). Flowering period: summer. Propagation: division/seed.

Lobelia cardinalis

One of the most startling red-flowered plants. Vivid blossoms borne in spires above beetroot-coloured foliage. There are a whole range of different coloured hybrids available with both green and maroon leaves. Height: 60-90cm (2-3ft). Spread: 30-45cm (1-1½ft). Flowering period: summer. Propagation: division/seed.

Primula candelabra hybrids

Early summer-flowering primulas with tiered whorls of multicoloured blossoms above coarse cabbagy leaves. There is a whole range of both species and named varieties in separate colours. Height: 60-75cm (2-2½ft). Spread: 30-40cm (1-1½ft). Flowering period: summer. Propagation: division/seed.

choosing plants

It is always preferable to choose aquatic plants from a specialist nurseryman, or alternatively from a garden centre which has an aquatic plant department which is stocked by a specialist grower. Ideally all marginal plants and waterlilies should be pot grown. Never purchase waterlilies or other aquatic plants which are floating loosely around in a sales tank. They will already have started to deteriorate. Bare-rooted aquatic plants are only satisfactory if received freshly lifted from the nursery.

Some garden centres and pet stores offer pre-packed aquatics, particularly submerged and floating plants. If these are sealed in polythene and hung on a peg board, give them a wide berth. They heat up quickly and spoil.

This also happens sometimes with submerged aquatics which are stocked loose in bunches in a tank. To check whether submerged plants are likely to be a good buy, look at the lead weight around the base of the bunch of cuttings. Black marks on the stems in the vicinity of the foliage indicates that the plant has been bunched for at least a week and that the lead strip is probably causing the stems to rot at the point where they are held together. Such plants should be avoided.

1 *Bog garden plants should be well clothed with unblemished foliage.*

2 *This hosta represents good value. When removed from the pot, it will be readily divisible.*

3 *A well-grown plant should display healthy foliage and also be capable of flowering successfully.*

4 *Plants should be established in their pots and not starved.*

5 *It is important that plants are free from pests and display only healthy undamaged foliage.*

Right: *For a garden pool to be a success, it is important to choose a range of aquatic plants which will create a harmonious balance. These plants should all have had the best possible start in life.*

Iris

Hosta

Astilbe

Stipa

Lysimachia

Lobelia

Above: *These plants show good husbandry. They are all growing healthily with no signs of pests and diseases. The containers are clean and topped off with a fresh layer of gravel and all are of reliable varieties.*

Right: *All the qualities of a good plant are visible here – healthy foliage, a full-sized flower and well presented container topped with gravel.*

Left: *A plant to avoid – starved and in an inadequate container competing with a mass of seedling weeds*

soils and composts

The soil or compost that is used for growing pond plants not only has a considerable influence upon their growth and performance, but also upon the clarity of the water in the pond. Healthy aquatic plants require a balance of nutrients in order to prosper, but these have to be available in such a form that the plants can readily assimilate them, without any leaching into the water. When nutrients become freely available in the water, they can be readily used by submerged plants, and when in excess, by green water-discolouring algae too. The successful balance of a water garden depends upon the aquatic plants having a suitable medium in which to grow whereby there are sufficient nutrients available for their well-being, but not for the undesirable lower forms of plant life, like slimes and algae, to prosper.

Aquatic planting composts are the most expensive growing mediums, but they do have the advantage of being balanced for successful pond plant cultivation, the nutrients being available in a slow-release form which does not readily disperse into the water. However, good clear garden soil, especially if of a medium or heavy nature, can be converted into a suitable growing medium for all aquatic plants.

Good clean garden soil is a viable alternative to aquatic planting compost. Any medium to heavy soil is suitable providing that it has not been dressed recently with artificial fertilizer. Sieve it well to remove any sticks and stones or water-polluting organic material.

Below: A balanced pond environment and healthy plants result from the use of properly prepared growing medium. There should be sufficient nutrients for the plants, without encouraging green algal bloom.

SOIL TEXTURE

1 Take some heavy garden soil from a part of the garden which has not recently received fertilizer. Dry thoroughly and break it down so that it can be spooned into an empty jar. Fill to within 2.5cm (1in) of the top.

2 Fill the jar to the top with clean tap water, allowing the dry soil particles to soak it up thoroughly. There will be considerable bubbling as the water drives out the air between the crumbs of soil.

3 Replace the lid and shake the jar thoroughly so that the soil particles are turned into a muddy slurry. The consistency of the contents should be like very runny chocolate with no discernible soil crumb structure evident.

4 Leave the jar undisturbed and allow the contents to settle out. Sand settles first, followed by clay, then clear water with organic matter floating on the top. 50 per cent clay content is the minimum requirement for aquatic plants.

planting and containers

It is important that pond plants have sufficient opportunity to develop a good root system without becoming over-crowded. Of all the plants that are grown in the decorative garden, aquatic plants unquestionably have the lustiest root growth. For this reason they are best grown in containers where they can be prevented from straying into one another, a particular benefit when routine division of the rootstocks takes place. Entangled neighbours can be a nightmare when the time comes to separate one from another.

Aquatic plants are unlike other garden plants for they do not grow well in ordinary plant pots. It is true that plants will prosper for a short time, but before the end of the season they will go into decline, irrespective of the compost. There needs to be an ability for the roots of the plants to escape into the water and for the compost to be effectively ventilated by direct exposure to the water through the sides of a lattice-work basket. In a closed pot, within 12 to 18 months the compost will turn blue or black and smell very unpleasant.

There are a wide range of aquatic planting baskets available, and although they are more expensive than pots or similar containers, they are an excellent investment and ensure that pond plants develop to their full potential.

Planting containers range from micromesh and traditional lattice-work and hessian arrangements to fabric planting bags.

PLANTING IN A BASKET

1 *Prepared soil or aquatic planting compost is put into the basket. Those with wide mesh sides should be lined with hessian to prevent soil spillage.*

2 *Prepare the plant by removing at least three-quarters of the foliage. Shorten back the root growth. A plant which is disturbed during its growing season dies back anyway, so removing excess growth works to its advantage and ensures rapid re-establishment.*

3 *For marginal aquatics multiple plantings are to be prepared. Three or four plants to each basket. Firm the plants in well and top up with compost as necessary. An initial watering settles the compost and drives out any air.*

Above: *Congested plantings of marginal and bog garden plants like irises require regular dividing and re-planting.*

4 *Top off the planting with a generous layer of well-washed pea gravel. This prevents soil spillage and fish disturbance.*

6 *The completed planting should be thoroughly watered before being placed in position in the pond. This drives out all the air and settles the compost.*

5 *With planting complete, surplus hessian from the lining of the basket should be trimmed off neatly with a pair of scissors.*

natural planting

There are occasions when planting directly into the pool is desirable. This is mostly when the pool has a natural soil bottom, or alternatively there is a liner sandwiched between the excavated shape and a generous layer of soil. In both cases the control of the spread of the plants has to be by soil sculpting. This is the varying of the internal levels of the pool so that only plants of certain kinds can grow. For example, if there is a shallow area of water 15cm (6in) deep where typha is flourishing, and the pool profile suddenly drops to 60cm (24in), the typha becomes restricted as it cannot survive in a 60cm (24in) depth of water. Thus the edge of the planting and its ultimate shape can be determined by the line of excavation between the 15cm (6in) and 60cm (24in) depths. The growth of the typha follows the area where the depth falls away.

It is quite possible to push bare-rooted plants into the mud on the floor of a naturally lined pool and for them to quickly establish. However, a much better start is achieved if initial plantings are made with an aquatic planting compost or prepared soil, the plants being wrapped in a textile which slowly deteriorates, but from which their roots can escape.

PLANTING A SOIL ROLL

1 *Where a natural-looking controlled planting is required, soil rolls made from old stockings or tights can be utilized. Fill the detached legs with a suitable compost.*

2 *Prepare plants of vigorous marginal aquatics for planting. Make small holes in the fabric, just sufficient to permit the roots to be pushed through and into the compost. Plant several plants of the same species in the roll.*

3 *The plants should be positioned 15 to 20cm (6-8in) apart so that they can quickly intermingle and develop into a solid mass of vegetation. The roots should soon engulf the roll.*

4 *Here plants of flowering rush,* Butomus umbellatus, *and the blue flowered* Mimulus ringens *have been established in the same roll. They have similar growth rates and flower in visual harmony.*

1 Planting in an earth-bottomed pool can be assisted by the use of hessian wraps. Take a bare-rooted plant, add aquatic planting compost and place on a hessian square.

2 Wrap the rootball up, securing it like a small parcel. Soak it thoroughly in water to drive out the air before lowering it into its permanent position in the pond.

3 Plants planted in hessian wraps are a perfect solution for the earth-bottomed pool. The roots penetrate the hessian and establish quickly into surrounding soil. Within a couple of seasons the hessian rots away without having impaired the development of the plants.

Above: *Reeds such as typhas are much loved residents of the wildlife pond and require thoughtful planting if their naturally invasive behaviour is to be controlled without stunting their growth.*

planting a waterlily

Waterlilies are not only the most decorative and important aquatic plants, but also the longest-lived and most expensive acquisitions for the pool. When purchasing a waterlily the cost is likely to be as much as a young decorative garden tree and the prospect of longevity much the same, although a waterlily does require regularly dividing.

The growth of every plant reflects the soil in which it is growing and for waterlilies this is particularly true, for they are gross feeders. This demand for nutrient used to be met by the liberal use of well-rotted animal manure or decomposing turf and many old gardening books made this recommendation. The problem with this was that

although the waterlilies prospered, so too did the various slimes and algaes which discolour pond water. The pool was a permanent nutrient-rich environment over which the gardener had no control.

Waterlilies are now widely sold growing in containers and often these can be introduced directly to the pool where they will grow away for a season without requiring any attention. Even if they require immediate re-potting, container-grown waterlilies are still the best option for the newcomer to water gardening and by using a balanced planting compost the requirements of the plants and the continued clarity of the water are both addressed.

PREPARING AND PLANTING A WATERLILY

2 *Remove all surplus fibrous root growth to within 1cm (0.4in) of the crown of the plant. Such roots are highly perishable and will not re-establish. By cutting off the old fibrous roots, fresh growth is stimulated which will make rapid and unimpeded progress. Pare back any dead tissue on the main crown.*

3 *All surface foliage and developing flower buds should be removed, the stems being cut back close to the main crown. If allowed to remain, the majority of surface floating foliage will in any event become yellow and die. In the meantime it can serve as an undesirable buoyancy aid and lift the plant out of its basket.*

1 *Select a strong-growing crown from a clump of waterlilies and remove any old or dying root system. As most waterlilies grow, they push out new creeping root systems, and the starchy remains of the old are of no further value.*

4 *The ideal waterlily crown should consist of a solid portion of starchy root system with a strong growing point with vigorous spear-like underwater shoots. Embryo flower buds can remain as these may develop into blossoms in favourable growing conditions.*

5 *Prepare a large planting basket with a suitable growing medium and plant the waterlily firmly in the centre. Water the compost to drive out the air.*

6 *Top-dress the container with washed pea gravel to reduce soil spillage and disturbance by fish once it is placed into the pool. Water again thoroughly.*

7 *Newly planted waterlilies can be placed on the floor of the pool in their final positions. They will rapidly establish themselves, producing a mass of fibrous roots and both submerged and floating foliage. Planted before mid-summer, a reasonable show of flowers can be expected in the first season.*

Above: *Waterlilies need periodic lifting, dividing and replanting. The first sign of crowding is when the central group of leaves starts climbing out of the water.*

division of a crowded marginal

Pond plants grow very quickly and marginal aquatics in particular require dividing often if they are to maintain the best quality flowers and foliage. In some cases this is as often as every second season. Division is also necessary with named varieties to guarantee that when propagated they are true to type. Seed-raised individuals from named varieties rarely come true.

Unlike plants in an herbaceous border which can be lifted and divided at any time during the dormant season, aquatic plants have to be divided during the spring. They can also be divided during the summer growing season, but in order for this to be carried out successfully the foliage and root systems have to be quite severely cut back. This then impairs the display, whereas if division takes place just as the plants start into growth, they develop unimpeded and flower satisfactorily that season.

With all aquatic plants it is essential to choose the young vigorous outer growths for replanting. The inner woody portions, although often appearing to be more substantial, rarely have the vigour exhibited by outer growths and generally produce a second-class display.

Right: Crowded marginal aquatics like these calthas must be regularly divided and replanted to maintain their quality.

DIVISION AND REPLANTING

2 *Remove all the roots to within 2 to 3cm (about 1in) of the crown. These are highly perishable and are in any event likely to die back.*

3 *Remove all the adult foliage with a sharp knife. The mature leaves of transplanted aquatics usually collapse and fade. It is best to give the new plant a fresh start.*

1 *Clump-forming marginal pond plants like this double flowered marsh marigold, Caltha palustris 'Flore Pleno', must be treated ruthlessly, but carefully. It will create a large number of divisions, each of which will be the same as the adult plant. Only use the very best divisions for replanting.*

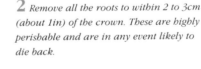

4 *Plants such as marsh marigolds will often divide into numerous young plantlets or divisions. Any shoot with a small crown and roots can be planted and will ultimately become a worthwhile specimen. For immediate replanting in the decorative pond, only use the more vigorous and larger young divisions. Make sure that they are of uniform size.*

5 *Use a specially prepared aquatic planting compost or good clean garden soil and fill the container to within 2 to 3cm (about 1in) of the top. This container is made from a rot-proof fabric and is sufficient to accommodate three plants. When planting make sure that the compost is firm.*

6 *Top-dress the compost with a layer of washed pea gravel and water well to drive out any air from the compost before lowering the container into the pond.*

7 *During the late spring and summer marginal plants which are divided re-establish themselves very quickly, many of the mid- to late summer flowering varieties making a reasonable show the same season. These calthas show the benefit of removing old foliage before division, new growth appearing within three or four weeks of division.*

fertilizing plants

Pond plants by their very nature are vigorous growers and heavy feeders. They require fertilizing at least once every season, but this has to be done in such a way that it benefits the plants and does not leach out into the water where it can encourage the development of a green algal bloom. The requirements of the first season after planting can be overcome by selecting a suitable well-balanced aquatic planting compost. Such a compost should contain sufficient nutrients to allow lusty growth for an entire season with no requirement for feeding until early the following summer. Most specialist-manufactured aquatic planting composts are well formulated and provide the likely nutritional requirements of all aquatic plants.

The pool itself will yield nutrients too, both from the inevitable decomposition of aquatic vegetation as well as the deposits from fish. However, in a well-balanced pool this will be insufficient to sustain the kind of growth and flowering that we expect from decorative pond plants if water clarity is to also be assured. The careful use of selected artificial fertilizers is desirable.

MAKING BONEMEAL PILLS

Aquatic plant fertilizer is available in small plastic sachets with perforations which permit the absorption of water. The sachet is pressed into the compost next to each plant.

1 *Take wet clay and mould it into small balls. Add up to 25 per cent by volume of bonemeal or fishmeal, rolling the material into the ball.*

2 *Place the fertilizer pill into the compost next to the plant. Nutrients will be slowly released into the compost without polluting the water.*

Left: *There are several standard pill-like slow-release fertilizers which can be used for aquatic plants in the same way as for shrubs and border subjects.*

Right: *Pond plants are gross feeders and require regular fertilizing if they are to maintain their quality and vigour. Over-fertilizing encourages the growth of algae.*

FEEDING PLANTS

All aquatic plants require nourishment, but not all demand formal feeding. Both submerged and floating aquatics derive their nutrients directly from the water, in the case of submerged plants their root systems performing an anchoring role rather than one which yields up nutrients. In the main they are foliar feeders and extract nutrients from the water rather than the growing medium. Thus in the well-maintained pond where plants and livestock are established in harmony, all the nourishment required comes from the water, at the same time creating conditions which water-discolouring algae find hard to tolerate.

Above: *When fertilizer leaches into the water, slimes and algae become a problem, so keep it contained within the compost adjacent to the roots of the plants.*

Waterlilies, deep-water aquatics and marginal plants on the other hand benefit from regular feeding. These derive their nourishment principally from the growing medium. While this should be enriched for the benefit of the plants, it should be done in such a way that there is minimal leaching into the water. When fertilizer is rapidly soluble or escapes into the water, then a green algal bloom follows which obscures pond life.

planting bog plants

Unlike marginal and deep-water aquatic plants, those of the bog garden must be planted during the traditional planting season, from autumn until late spring. Pot- or container-grown plants can be planted at any time but the best results are obtained from a dormant planting of a bare-rooted plant lifted straight from the nursery.

It is important that bog plants have proper boggy conditions and not just damp ones, so correct provision should be made which ensures that the bog garden does not sit permanently under water, but that the soil is saturated, yet without even occasional surface puddles.

Often a bog garden is contrived as an element next to a pond and is constructed at the same time, the water from the pond seeping through a permeable barrier and maintaining the moisture level of the bog garden at the desired level. This is the ideal, for the conditions in the bog garden can be readily controlled.

Alternatively the bog area can be built alongside the pool with its own water supply. This is less desirable, but in most cases is the only way in which a boggy area can be established adjacent to an already established pool.

Above: *A bog garden or moist streamside provides a home for perennials which cannot be grown in permanent standing water.*

CREATING A BOG AREA

1 *A bog garden can be created as part of a pool at the same time as its construction, or as a separate entity, as here.*

2 *An excavation is lined with pool liner and drainage holes created with a fork.*

3 *The drainage holes help to prevent winter waterlogging as does a generous layer of up to 20cm (6in) of pea gravel. This should be raked out over the floor of the excavation prior to filling the area with soil. The gravel helps to keep the roots of the plants away from standing water.*

4 Although a bog garden that is created in a lined excavation is likely to be mostly wet, it is possible during dry periods for the lining to have the effect of creating a dry contained area of soil. To combat this, introduce a length of irrigation hose.

Below: *A small bog garden displaying the diversity of flower and foliage offered by moisture-loving perennials. These consist of irises, hostas, sensitive fern, primulas, mimulus, lobelia and astilbe.*

5 Add soil and fill the excavation to the top. A richly organic soil is to be preferred. As this is added, position the length of hosepipe in the lower layer. In dry periods this can be connected to the tap and so will ensure constant moisture. A perforated hose is ideal for this purpose.

6 Bog garden plants are ideally planted bare-rooted in the spring just as they are showing signs of growth. Pot-grown specimens can be planted at any time of the year. If the rootball is congested, it should be disrupted at planting time.

waterlily propagation from eyes

Waterlilies grow from fleshy creeping rootstocks. In a natural pond these spread through the mud on the pool floor and periodically produce fresh clumps of growth from large bud-like crowns. Such growths have developed from eyes. These are dormant buds which appear with varying frequency along the rootstocks of mature waterlilies. Most eyes do not sprout and grow into new plants while part of a long-established root system, but once removed they can quickly be encouraged into growth and will soon become vigorous young plants which in many cases will flower during their second season.

The fleshy part of the rootstock of a waterlily is really a stem with buds and the removal of dormant buds is akin to taking cuttings. Like the cuttings of other plants, being vegetative they always come completely true to type. The eyes vary in their appearance, but mostly they will have produced a couple of small leaves and perhaps an occasional adventitious root. Varieties derived from *Nymphaea tuberosa* are slightly different. The eyes of these are like rounded lumps or nodules and appear attached to the rootstock, rather than as a part of it. They are quite brittle and easily dislodged.

EYE PROPAGATION

2 Trim each eye so that it comprises little more than a dynamic-looking dormant bud, removing any spears of foliage or vestiges of root.

1 Remove eyes from the rootstock with a sharp knife with a sliver of starchy tissue attached. The eyes will vary in size and stages of development from dormant buds to young sprouting growths. Each has the capability to develop into a viable plant if handled carefully.

A mature waterlily has a fleshy rootstock along which are dormant buds or eyes. If removed, these can be rooted and established as young plants.

3 Plant each eye individually in a small pot using a prepared aquatic planting compost or good clean finely sieved garden soil. Allow 1cm (0.4in) for a top dressing of pea gravel.

4 *Place the pots into a bowl of water with the leaves just over the top of the pot. As the eyes break into growth, raise the level slightly to permit the extension of the leaf stalks. Keep the plants in full light and regularly remove any filamentous algae.*

5 *After five or six weeks the plants will start to develop and become recognizable as young waterlilies. Gradually increase the water level in the container and allow the plants to grow on until they fill the small pots with roots. At this stage they are ready to plant out permanently in the garden pond.*

Right: *Although it is possible to raise seedlings from waterlilies like 'Pink Sensation', the progeny are never true to type and usually inferior. Propagation by eyes guarantees that the young plants are exactly like the parent.*

division propagation – reeds and rushes

The division of aquatic plants is one of the principal and most successful methods of propagation. For the majority of reeds and rushes it is the only method that is likely to work for the home gardener. Some reeds and rushes do produce seed, but its germination is erratic. Its viability is also very dependant upon the season and it can mostly only be obtained by gathering fresh from growing plants. Seed merchants rarely offer such seed. In many cases it does not come true, particularly with mutants like the distinctively marked zebra rush, *Schoenoplectus tabernaemontani* 'Zebrinus'.

Division offers the best solution providing that it is undertaken in the spring just as fresh growth is emerging. Making divisions just as the parent plant is coming into active growth more or less guarantees that the young divisions will grow away strongly once detached.

Amongst the reeds and rushes are a number of different rootstocks, ranging from the vigorous creeping *Typha latifolia,* with viciously pointed rhizomes as thick as a finger, to the congested clusters of roots and bulbils of *Butomus umbellatus* and the straightforward fibrous root system of the *Juncus* species. All are easily divisible providing a small growing point is retained.

Many reeds and rushes have very vigorous root systems which are sometimes not contained by a micromesh planting basket. All can be increased by division.

PROPAGATING FLOWERING RUSH

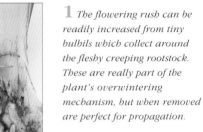

1 *The flowering rush can be readily increased from tiny bulbils which collect around the fleshy creeping rootstock. These are really part of the plant's overwintering mechanism, but when removed are perfect for propagation.*

2 *The bulbils look like large grains of cereal, but are tight buds just waiting to burst into growth. Many have roots present. Plant individually in small pots in a good aquatic planting compost.*

3 *After a couple of months a bulbil will have produced a pot-full of roots and become well established with extensive leaf development. Once the pot is congested with roots, the young plant can be removed and planted in its permanent position in a planting basket.*

Above: *There is a wide variety of reeds, rushes and aquatic grasses. While some can be increased from seed, all can be propagated by division.*

PROPAGATING RUSHES

1 *Division is the only way to propagate the corkscrew rush and ensure that the twisted characteristic is retained. Take a sharp knife and separate rooted portions.*

2 *As this plant is a mutation, it is important that only divisions which clearly show the corkscrew-type characteristic are retained. The straight stemmed division will revert to the common type if potted up.*

3 *Remove the foliage to within 2 or 3cm (about 1in) of the crown and similarly trim the roots back hard. Pot individual divisions in pots in a prepared aquatic planting compost. Stand in shallow water.*

division propagation – other marginals

While there are specialist root systems and forms of division, largely amongst the reeds and rushes, the majority of marginal aquatic plants are lifted and divided in much the same way as their herbaceous border relatives. The main difference is that aquatic plants must be divided during the growing season, between late spring and late summer, whereas those of the border are usually dealt with during the autumn and winter.

For most marginal plants spring division is best, just as the new season's growth is appearing. By doing this, young plants can have a whole growing season before them. Also those that are planted back into the pond for display purposes have the prospect of producing a reasonable show if re-established before the summer.

There are exceptions, notably irises. While these can be successfully lifted and divided in the spring, doing so ruins their early summer display. It is much better to follow tradition and to lift and divide aquatic irises immediately after flowering. Thus the current season's display is assured and the divisions which are placed immediately after flowering are sufficiently well established to make a good display the next summer. Indeed, they are often sizeable clumps again at flowering time.

DIVISION OF IRISES

1 *Irises, or other similar marginal plants such as* Acorus, *should be separated into individual fans of leaves and have both roots and foliage trimmed back.*

2 *The individual plant divisions should be potted in aquatic planting compost and stood with water just above the rims of the pots. After six to eight weeks they can be planted out.*

DIVISION OF CLUMP-FORMING MARGINALS

1 *Many marginal plants, such as* Mimulus ringens, *grow in tight clumps and can be lifted periodically and separated into individual plants.*

2 *The foliage should be cut back to within 5 to 10cm (2 to 4in) of the base and the roots reduced to 2-3cm (about 1in). Pot individually in small pots containing aquatic planting compost and stand in water which is just above the rims of the pots.*

Above: Named varieties of marginals like the variegated Iris can only be successfully propagated by division.

DIVIDING DWARF MARGINALS

1 *There are several short-growing plants, like* Sisyrinchium angustifolium, *which produce myriad tiny divisions which require treating like seedlings in a seed tray.*

2 *The individual divisions should have the foliage and roots reduced to about half their length. They should then be pricked out into a seed tray in an aquatic planting compost.*

3 *After a couple of months standing in a tray of shallow water, they develop enough to be potted individually in aquatic planting compost topped with pea gravel.*

stem cuttings

Stem cuttings are a traditional method of increasing a wide array of garden plants. They can equally well be utilized for many aquatic plants, especially marginal and bog garden subjects. As the plants which we grow in our ponds are often very different from those of the herbaceous bed and border, it is often unclear to the newcomer to water gardening as to which can be increased by this method.

Irrespective of the variety, there is a good general rule which can be applied to determine whether a plant will root from a stem cutting. If the plant has leaves with veins in a net arrangement, e.g. *Mimulus*, it can be increased from a cutting. If the leaves have parallel veins, e.g. *Iris*, then stem cuttings are out. To confirm suitability further check with the flowers. All plants producing blossoms with three, six or multiples of three petals cannot be rooted from stem cuttings, those with four, five or more petals, but which are not divisible by three, can all be increased from cuttings. This is a useful tip in determining the viability of this propagation technique with other garden plants as well.

Of course the plant to be propagated has to produce suitable short stems from which to make cuttings and these should ideally be fresh and healthy with no intention of flowering. With most aquatics such shoots are usually evident during late spring.

CREEPING STEM CUTTINGS

1 The fact that the bog arum, Calla palustris, *has a creeping stem does not mean that the opportunities for propagation are limited. The main growing point can be removed and planted individually, the long creeping leafless stem being converted into propagation material.*

2 Select firm growth and cut sections of stem 3 to 5cm (up to 2in) long, each with a fresh green dormant bud in the centre. Remove any stem scales and vestiges of root.

3 Pot each stem section horizontally with the bud uppermost in individual pots filled with aquatic compost. Water thoroughly.

4 Place the pots into a bowl with the water just over the pot rims. If prior watering was thorough, any escape of air from the compost should not displace the cuttings.

5 Cuttings taken during late spring or early summer will have developed into adult plants by late summer.

TRADITIONAL STEM CUTTINGS

1 *Creeping plants like brooklime,* Veronica beccabunga, *can be easily and quickly increased by short stem cuttings taken from late spring until mid-summer.*

2 *Make short jointed cuttings for preference, always severing them at a leaf joint. This is the part of the stem where the cells that are stimulated into root production are most numerous. Trim the lower leaves and remove any flowers.*

3 *Place the cuttings around the edge of a pot in aquatic planting compost or finely sieved soil and stand in a bowl with water just covering the pot rims.*

4 *After three or four week the cuttings will have rooted and will be well established in the pot. They then start to become crowded and, if not separated out, will grow into a great tangle and thus be spoiled.*

5 *Separate out the plants and pot them individually in an aquatic planting compost. In order to develop bushy growth, the tops of the cuttings should be pinched out at leaf joints. The buds in the angles of all the leaves will then break out and produce fresh shoots. These in turn can be pinched back to encourage a dense habit of growth.*

Above: *The only reliable method of increasing the bog bean,* Menyanthes trifoliata, *is by stem cuttings using the same method as employed for* Calla palustris. *This should be done in early summer after flowering.*

propagating submerged plants

Submerged aquatic plants are for the most part increased from cuttings, although there are a couple of species which are clump-forming and increased by division. These are common hair grass, *Eleocharis acicularis*, and *Isoetes lacustris*, a short-growing rush-like plant which is not widely cultivated. These two are merely divided into separate plantlets and replanted in the same way as marginal subjects. All other submerged aquatics are increased from stem cuttings which are made into bunches fastened together at the base with a short strip of lead.

The cuttings of submerged plants should all be taken from the current season's growth. Propagation can therefore take place at any time from late spring until late summer. Although taking cuttings is a method of increasing plant stock, with many species it is part of a maintenance programme, for after a season established clumps look very weary. However, being quick-growing, fresh young stock can be used as replacement each season if cuttings are taken as early in the spring as possible.

WARNING
An aquatic environment provides a great opportunity for alien plant species to spread and smother less vigorous natives. Pools and streams are often very delicately balanced in nature and easily disrupted. One such plant which is now threatening wildlife areas is the Australian stonecrop, Crassula helmsii.

Spring growth is always the easiest to propagate. That produced towards the end of the summer will often become brittle and be difficult to bunch, especially growth which has recently flowered.

PROPAGATING A SUBMERGED PLANT

1 *Remove established growth from the pool which has young shoots at least 5cm (2in) long. Wash the vegetation thoroughly and remove any clinging filamentous algae.*

2 *Make individual cuttings from this season's growth. Fasten these together at the base with a narrow strip of lead.*

3 *Insert the bunches of cuttings into a basket of aquatic planting compost. Ensure that the lead around each bunch is buried or it will rot through the stems and the tops of the cuttings will float to the surface.*

4 *Top off the planting with a generous layer of well-washed pea gravel. This helps to prevent soil spillage into the water and deters the fish from disturbing the basket.*

5 *Position the basket in the pool having first watered it thoroughly to drive all the air out of the compost. This prevents violent bubbling and the disturbance of the cuttings.*

6 *After a month, the cuttings will have become well established and a container of lush submerged vegetation will result.*

Above: *Submerged aquatic plants depend upon regular propagation and replacement to remain strong and of vigorous growth. This is essential to maintain a healthy, well-balanced aquatic environment for the fish and other aquatic life to enjoy.*

raising from seed

Many aquatic plants can be successfully raised from seed, although it is wise to check first to see whether any other propagation method is appropriate. Seed raising can produce a considerable numbers of plants, but it often takes a lot longer for them to become of sufficient size for planting out compared with those grown from cuttings or division.

Seed-raised plants are only of species or strains. For the most part named varieties of garden plants, whether aquatic or not, do not come true to type from seed. There are occasional exceptions, such as the bog garden primula,

Primula japonica 'Postford White'. That is not to say that good seed-raised strains of aquatics are in any way inferior; indeed amongst the mimulus the commercial selections are mostly far superior to the named varieties which have to be increased from cuttings.

Often the seed of aquatic plants has to be gathered from growing plants. Few seed companies stock pond plant seed, as in most cases its viability is limited. The best results are achieved by sowing seeds collected directly from the parent plant immediately it has ripened.

RAISING AQUATICS FROM SEED

1 *True aquatic plants can often be raised from seed, but almost without exception this must be freshly gathered on the point of ripening and sown immediately. Bog garden seeds are more conventional and some, like mimulus and primula, are available commercially and are sown in early spring. Use a good seed compost and distribute the seed sparingly over the surface of the seed tray.*

2 *Cover the seeds with a thin layer of compost. For small seeds the compost should ideally be passed through a fine sieve. It is important to firm the compost gently to ensure that the seeds do not float away or become redistributed when the seed tray is placed in water. Water the tray gently from above before placing it in standing water so that any air in the compost is driven out.*

3 *Bog garden seeds like mimulus should be subjected to wet conditions, but must not be submerged. Place the seed tray in a deeper tray with sufficient water so that the level outside is equivalent to the surface level of the compost within the tray. An excess of water will rot the seeds.*

Right: Most species and mixed strains of bog garden plants can be raised successfully from seed, including candelabra primulas like the crimson flowered Primula japonica.

4 *When the seedlings have germinated and the first rough leaves are showing, they should be separated and pricked out into a seed tray to grow on.*

5 *Once the seed tray becomes full of roots and the foliage is a congested mass, the young plants can be lifted carefully and either potted individually or planted directly outside.*

root cuttings and plantlets

It often surprises gardeners that many herbaceous plants can be increased quickly and successfully from root cuttings and plantlets. Amongst the plants that we popularly grow in our water gardens, it is the bog garden subjects that are most amenable to this form of propagation. Primulas are particularly agreeable to root-cutting propagation, so too *Houttuynia*, although this spreads so quickly that plantlet divisions are a better option when only a few plants are required. As with stem cuttings, the propagation of plants from root cuttings and division guarantees that the progeny are true to type.

The principle which permits root cuttings to be successful is similar to that of suckering. Many plants have roots which have latent buds that remain dormant until the root is damaged, typically seen as suckering. By removing pieces of root from plants which have dormant buds, the buds are stimulated into growth.

***Right:** Candelabra primulas are excellent plants to increase from either root cuttings or plantlets. Root cuttings are usually taken during the winter, while root divisions are made immediately after flowering during summer.*

TAKING ROOT CUTTINGS

1 *Lift a suitable parent plant during the winter or immediately after flowering and remove fleshy roots. These should not be wispy like string, nor any thicker than a pencil. A middle size is ideal. Once the roots have been removed, the parent plant can be firmed back in its permanent position. It should re-establish quickly.*

2 *Take the fresh roots and cut them into lengths of up to 2cm (¾in). This will ensure that there is at least one dormant bud present on each section which can break into growth. Discard thin stringy portions of root. Do not permit the cuttings to dry out and plant them immediately.*

3 *Prepare a seed tray with a multipurpose potting compost and place the root sections evenly and horizontally across the surface. This will allow plenty of room for the young plantlets to develop unimpeded.*

4 *Cover the root cuttings with compost, then firm and water. Place the tray in a cold frame for the best results. Root cuttings do not respond well to high temperatures.*

SEPARATING PLANTLETS

1 *Some bog garden plants, such as primulas, can be lifted straight after flowering, have their foliage cut hard back and then be divided.*

2 *Separate out the tiniest individuals. These will eventually make new plants. Trim back the roots and pot the small divisions individually in potting compost. Plant the larger divisions directly outdoors.*

storing plants overwinter

The majority of hardy aquatic plants survive the winter without any difficulty. However, there are benefits to be obtained through making some provisions for storage of their winter growth in order that young plants can have a head start in the spring. This particularly applies to floating aquatics.

Most floating species produce winter buds or turions and if these can be afforded some winter protection, they can be started into growth much earlier in the spring. Under natural conditions turions fall to the bottom of the pool at the approach of autumn. Here they remain until the spring sun warms up the water when they return to the surface and grow out into new plants. In some instances, such as frogbit, *Hydrocharis morsus-ranae*, the winter stage is a tight bud reminiscent of a bulbil, whereas with others like the water chestnut, *Trapa natans*, it is seeds which are produced. In the pool it would be impossible to gather these to start into growth, but by overwintering them in a container with some water, early development can be assured if a little warmth is applied.

Other turions benefit from protection from winter predators, amongst them the sagittarias or arrowheads. These plants produce small turions like potatoes which are popularly known as duck potatoes and indeed are much-loved by wild fowl.

OVERWINTERING WATER HYACINTH

1 *Water hyacinth,* Eichhornia crassipes, *is not hardy in areas subject to frost. Select young vigorous plantlets for overwintering indoors. Discard old plants.*

2 *The water hyacinth does not overwinter well in deep water. It much prefers to remain in a shallow bowl in a muddy gruel. The bottom of the bowl should be covered with a generous layer of aquatic planting compost into which the plant can root if it desires. Keep in full light at a minimum temperature of 10°C (50°F).*

Ceratophyllum demersum *or bornwort produces small brush-like winter buds. Place a few of these in a jar of water with soil on the bottom and keep in the light so as to get some early growth.*

OVERWINTERING FAIRY MOSS

1 *Fairy moss,* Azolla filiculoides, *is a floating aquatic which is not reliably hardy. It often disappears for the winter and reappears during the late spring.*

2 *To ensure its survival and to guarantee some healthy growth early in the spring, it can be easily overwintered by being placed in a container of water with a layer of soil on the bottom in early autumn.*

3 *The container should be positioned in a well-lit place and kept at a minimum temperature of 5°C (41°F). Remove any mould that may occasionally develop.*

STORING TURIONS

1 *All arrowheads,* Sagittaria, *produce turions. These are vulnerable to wildlife, especially wild fowl. Arrowheads also benefit from kick-starting into early spring growth with a little protection. Turions can be removed from a mature plant in late summer.*

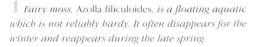

2 *Turions are highly perishable and should be stored in damp sand during the winter. Place them in layers in a jar and store in a cool frost-free place. They are removed in early spring and planted in pots until sprouting vigorously, when they can be planted out permanently.*

OVERWINTERING WATER LETTUCE

1 *Water lettuce,* Pistia stratiotes, *is an attractive tropical floating plant which spends the summer outdoors in the pool. It starts to suffer when the temperature drops below 10°C (50°F). The older plants are difficult to overwinter, so select vigorous young plantlets which are still attached to the parent and bring them indoors in early autumn.*

2 *Water lettuce is difficult to overwinter in deep water. It requires a bowl of water with a layer of soil on the bottom, plenty of light and a temperature of 18°C (64°F).*

routine maintenance

Whether or not your interests extend to fish, it is important to maintain good water quality and clarity. This is largely brought about by creating a balance between the various classes of plants and selecting a suitable type of compost, especially with regard to its component nutrients and their solubility.

Controlling blanket weed and green water

Algae is a problem for every pool owner, even it if is just for those two or three weeks in late spring when the water has warmed up, and the higher plants are not in active

growth and capable of providing sufficient competition. Aquatic algae occurs in many forms, but these can be divided primarily into free-floating and filamentous. The free-floating kinds swarm in great masses and give water the 'pea soup' effect. The filamentous kinds on the other hand appear as free-floating silkweed or spirogyra or else in thick mats known as blanket or flannel weed. Other species like the mermaid's hair cling to plants and baskets and often coat the walls of the pool as well.

There are no magical cures for the various algal problems and the best permanent solution is based upon the theory of a natural balance; plants both providing competition for mineral salts and creating shade beneath. Chemical controls are at the very best only temporary solutions, but can be very useful in the early life of a pool while the higher plants are becoming established. Elimination of water-discolouring algae at this stage allows more light to enter the water and consequently aids establishment of submerged plants.

Free-floating algae can be controlled relatively easily using a proprietary algaecide. Filamentous algae are more

Right: To ensure a long-lasting and happy balance within the pool and amongst the poolside vegetation, careful attention has to be paid to regular year-round care and maintenance.

difficult. While they can be killed with an algaecide, the dead algae must be removed from the water in order to prevent de-oxygenation which would suffocate the fish.

Coping with trees and leaves

One of the greatest maintenance problems for the pool owner are fallen leaves during the autumn. These blow around and collect in the pool causing problems for the fish as they decompose and de-oxygenate the water. In quantity they do little for water clarity, either causing discolouration, or eventually adding nutrients which further encourage the development of algae. Some leaves are extremely toxic, not to plants, but to fish and should be excluded by whatever means possible. These include those of the horse chestnut family *(Aesculus)*, which are particularly noxious as well as willows *(Salix)*, which have properties similar to aspirin which can harm the fish when they decompose in the pool.

The best way to protect a pool from falling leaves is with netting. Common recommendations are for netting the pool over completely; however, this is not only unsightly but can also damage the plants. It is much better to get some small mesh wire netting about 45cm (18in) high and to fasten this to stakes around the pool. This prevents most leaves from entering the water as the majority blow into the pool from the surrounding garden, rather than fall directly from tree into water. The netting serves as a barrier which they collect against.

YEAR-ROUND MAINTENANCE

Spring

- Pond plants can be planted.
- Divide waterlilies and marginal aquatics where necessary.
- Take cuttings from submerged plants, re-bunch and replant where necessary.
- When the pond requires cleaning, do so only during spring.
- Sow seeds of bog garden and aquatic plants which are available commercially.
- Take stem cuttings of appropriate marginal aquatics.
- Propagate waterlilies from eyes.
- Repot and renew compost of any appropriate plants which do not necessarily require dividing.

Summer

- Control filamentous algae by twisting out with a nail through a stick.
- Introduce new aquatic plants as required.
- Cut off the faded blossoms of marginal plants.
- Net off surplus floating growth of carpeting plants like fairy moss.
- Take stem cuttings of appropriate marginal plants.
- Fertilize the growing mediums of established waterlilies and marginal plants in early summer.
- Sow freshly collected seeds of aquatic plants.
- Control the exuberant growth of any aquatic plants.

Autumn

- Collect and store plantlets and turions of appropriate aquatics ready for the winter.
- Net the pool to keep out leaves.
- Cut back all faded aquatic plants, but do not cut hollow-stemmed marginals below water level or else they may rot.
- Take root cuttings of appropriate bog garden plants.

Winter

- Ensure an ice-free area on the pond to permit the escape of accumulated gases which may harm the fish.

caring for your wildlife

Even if you have little interest in fish, it is wise to introduce a few to a pond in order to control mosquito larvae and aquatic insect pests. Indeed, fish are the most reliable control of pests such as caddis fly larvae. It is not necessary to have many fish, nor to go to much trouble to look after them, for in a well-planted environment they will look after themselves. Indeed, they only require feeding when the plants are first becoming established. After that, they find plenty to eat, a well-balanced pool providing a varied natural diet.

Left: *Although growing pond plants may be the main objective of the water gardener, fish are a valuable adjunct to the pool, not only being visually attractive but also controlling aquatic insect pests and mosquitoes. Hardy varieties of goldfish are easy to keep.*

WATER QUALITY

The acidity or alkalinity of pond water is only of marginal importance in the cultivation of pond plants and the maintenance of a happy balance. Occasionally plants like the cotton grass, *Eriophorum angustifolium*, are encountered which do not tolerate alkaline conditions, but equally fairy moss, *Azolla filiculoides*, resents acid ones. There are test kits available from the garden centre, but much can be learned by careful pond observation.

Water soldiers, *Stratiotes aloides*, are fine indicators of water conditions. These floating plants become suspended beneath the water in acid conditions, but rise above it when the pH is alkaline. When neutral, they settle to a half-way existence which is what most pond owners prefer. Ramshorn snails are also fine indicators of water conditions. In alkaline water their shells are beautifully smooth, but in acid conditions they become pock-marked and pitted.

FISH CARE

For the pond owner who has no particular interest in fish, but appreciates the benefits that they can bring, the common goldfish is the cheapest, toughest and most reliable. Introduced into the pond during late spring or the early summer months, they will have settled down by the autumn and will pass through the winter happily.

The only winter consideration for their well-being comes during periods of prolonged freezing when the pool ices over. The fish will be hardy enough, but they may suffer from the accumulation of noxious gases created by decomposing organic matter on the floor of the pond which, if not permitted to escape into the air, can asphyxiate them. Make a hole in the ice by placing a pan of boiling water on the surface and allowing it to melt through. Never break the ice with a blunt instrument as this can concuss the fish.

Left: A pool can become a wildlife haven. Birds bathe in its margins and all manner of creatures use it as a watering hole. There are many creatures, such as the common toad, who will find sanctuary and perform a useful service in disposing of slugs and snails on its regular foray into the garden. Other aquatic life which is likely to arrive includes a variety of frogs and newts. All enhance the visual appeal of the water garden and contribute to its well-being.

Symptoms	Cause	Control
Surface layers of leaves and flowers of waterlilies stripped away. Small brown beetles and shiny black larvae present.	Waterlily beetle	In summer knock the creatures into the pool with a strong jet of water and allow the fish to devour them. Good pondside hygiene in autumn denies them a place to overwinter.
Floating foliage of any aquatic plant cut and shred, floating on water surface.	Brown china mark moth	Hand-pick larvae and net out all floating debris which may have larvae attached.
Pieces of floating foliage of any aquatic plant neatly removed.	Caddis flies	No cure, but a good fish population will keep the pest under control.
Badly damaged leaves of waterlilies, deep-water aquatics and some floating plants. Often jelly-like cylinders on the undersides of the leaves.	Greater pond snails	Hand-picking helps, but floating a fresh lettuce leaf overnight will capture many snails which can be removed and destroyed.
Foliage distorted. Masses of tiny black insects present on waterlily pads and the foliage of succulent marginal aquatics.	Waterlily aphid	Winter wash nearby plum and cherry trees to destroy overwintering populations. In summer wash aphids into the pool with a strong jet of water from a hosepipe. The fish will then devour them.

index

Picture Credits
Eric Crichton: 10, 13 lower, 17, 23, 24-25, 25, 42, 61. **John Glover:** 3, 4, 6, 7, 8, 9 (both), 11 left, 14 (both), 19, 21, 27, 28-29 (design: Jane Sweetser, Hampton Court Flower Show 1999), 30-31, 37, 39, 41, 45, 47 (design: Paul Dyer, Chelsea Flower Show 1999), 49, 55, 57, 62, 63. **S. and O. Mathews:** 5, 11 right, 12, 15, 22, 26 (both), 51, 53. **Plant Pictures World Wide:** 33, 35. **Neil Sutherland:** 1, 13 upper, 16 (both), 18, 20, 24.